GRIZZLY!

REAL-LIFE ANIMAL ATTACKS

GRIZZLY!

REAL-LIFE ANIMAL ATTACKS

Allen B. Ury

LOWELL HOUSE JUVENILE

LOS ANGELES

NTC/Contemporary Publishing Group

Published by Lowell House
A division of NTC/Contemporary Publishing Group, Inc.
4255 West Touhy Avenue
Lincolnwood (Chicago), Illinois 60646-1975 U.S.A.

Lowell House books can be purchased at special discounts when
ordered in bulk for premiums and special sales. Contact
Department CS at the following address:
NTC/Contemporary Publishing Group
4255 W. Touhy Avenue
Lincolnwood, IL 60646-1975
1-800-323-40900

ISBN: 0-7373-0042-6

Library of Congress Catalog Card Number: 98-067907

Roxbury Park is a division of
NTC/Contemporary Publishing Group, Inc.

Managing Director and Publisher: Jack Artenstein
Editor in Chief, Roxbury Park Books: Michael Artenstein
Director of Publishing Services: Rena Copperman
Editorial Assistant: Nicole Monastirsky
Interior Design: Victor Perry

Printed and bound in the United States of America

10 9 8 7 6 5 4 3 2 1

" For Rene & Robert —
Who know all too well that living
with a writer can be a real bear."

Contents

Introduction

We live in a dangerous world. Every year about 40,000 Americans are killed in automobile-related accidents. About that same number of our fellow citizens are killed annually by firearms, either by accident or

as the result of criminal activity. In 1996 approximately 1,500 people were killed in airplane crashes worldwide. And *millions* of Americans die less spectacular deaths each year from lifestyle-related illnesses such as heart disease and smoking-related cancers.

But there's another source of danger most people don't even consider in this modern, technological age. Yet it's one that's as old as life itself, one our species has had to contend with for much of its existence, and one that continues to make its presence known despite our best efforts to contain and control it. I'm speaking, of course, about animals.

The phrase "It's a jungle out there" is more than just a colorful saying about the often savage nature of daily human life. It's also a fitting description for the constant battle for survival being waged between human beings and the animal kingdom of which we remain an inseparable part. Yes, we can shelter ourselves in caves of steel, brick, and concrete; enclose our territories with barbed wire and defend them with firearms; and even attempt to domesticate wild beasts for food, companionship, and amusement. But despite our best efforts to reshape the world in our image, this thing we call "civilization" is the most delicate of constructs, and inevitably man and beast find themselves locked in mortal conflict. Whether in the mountains or the city, on land or in the water, against the greatest of land mammals or the tiniest of insects, our arrogance toward nature is constantly being tested by those forces we thought we had tamed, yet which refuse to conform to our definition of order.

In this book, I present some of the most interesting confrontations between man and beast to have occurred in the past decade. Some have taken place in the animals' native domain, and some in our own. The animals involved range from the great American grizzly bear to common house pets to the tiny fire ant. Many of these battles proved fatal for the people involved, while in other cases the human victims lived to tell the tale. And while some of these attacks appear to have been totally unprovoked, a good many were the direct result of human provocation.

Nature is an elegant thing, and nothing happens in it without a purpose. When animals do attack, it's most often for reasons of hunger or self-preservation, in defense of territory, or while protecting their young. (Humans, by contrast, are one of the few animals that kill just for the pure pleasure of it.) Knowing this, it becomes easier to see these animals not as brute forces of nature—and certainly not as "evil"—but merely as creatures going about their daily lives. Hopefully we'll be able to view them with a truer sense of awe, of fear, and even respect.

SECTION 1

FROM THE MOUNTAINS TO THE PRAIRIE

Animal Attacks in the Great Outdoors

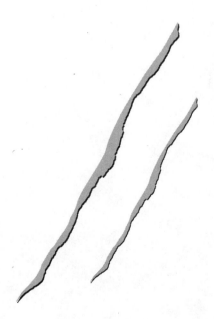

chapter 1

The Bear Facts

Bears are the largest carnivores in North America, and among the various species present on the continent, the grizzly is by far the most fierce—and the most feared. Also known as silvertip bears, grizzlies may grow to a height of 7 feet and weigh up to 850 pounds.

Like most other types of bears, including their close cousins, the black bears, grizzlies are actually omnivores and will eat virtually anything available, including fruits, nuts, and vegetables. However, the grizzly clearly has a preference for meat, particularly large game animals such as deer.

Contrary to popular myth, grizzlies, like other bears, don't "hug" their victims to death. Instead, they kill their prey through a combination of powerful swipes with their huge clawed paws and bites from their large, muscular jaws.

Grizzlies, which were nearly hunted to extinction during the nineteenth century, are today found principally in protected areas such as national parks and forests. Although bears tend to shun human contact, man and beast do occasionally come face to face. When such confrontations occur, the results are inevitably dramatic, often violent, and sometimes downright deadly.

SEVENTY-YEAR-OLD retiree Ken Larson of Murrells Inlet, South Carolina, had been warned about the presence of grizzly bears in Montana's Glacier National Park when he decided to go for a 4-mile hike on the morning of June 5, 1996. But he'd been assured by a park naturalist that Avalanche Lake Trail, which began about 10 miles from the Lake McDonald Lodge where he and his wife, Bonnie, were staying, was probably safe. No bears had recently been reported in the area.

As detailed in the August 9, 1996, issue of the *Los Angeles Times,* Larson began his hike around 6:30 A.M., as was his habit back home in South Carolina. Having read that bears tend to avoid humans if they have enough warning, he regularly shouted "Hello!" and "Yo ho!" to warn any potential predators of his presence.

Approximately 45 minutes into his walk, Larson realized that, sometime back, he had left the Avalanche Lake Trail and had somehow gotten onto Johns Lake Trail, a less-traveled path. Having reached the halfway point in his hike, he immediately turned around and began heading back.

Minutes later a huge, 300-pound grizzly bear appeared in the path no more than 20 feet away. And it was bounding straight for him.

Larson jumped off the trail in search of shelter, but the bear was quickly upon him. It struck him across the back of his head, cutting a bloody 6-inch-long gash in his scalp.

Park visitors are routinely warned that, if attacked by a bear, the best course of action is to simply play dead. Larson did exactly this, but the bear continued to bat him about, then savagely bit his left leg, breaking his tibia and tearing a golf ball-size chunk of flesh from his calf.

The entire attack is believed to have lasted less than a minute, after which the grizzly apparently lost interest and padded off into the woods. Although in great pain, Larson remained as quiet as possible as he listened for any sounds that might indicate the bear's return. When he believed the danger had finally passed, he struggled to his feet and limped weakly back to his car, a journey that took just 20 minutes, but which to Larson must have seemed like an eternity.

As if things weren't bad enough, Larson was shocked to discover when he arrived at his car that his keys had fallen out of his pocket, presumably sometime during the battle. Fortunately, another car soon arrived, driven by Kim and Tori Ziemann, sisters who had summer jobs in the park. They wrapped Larson's bloody head wound in a shirt and drove him directly to the nearest nurse's station. From there he was helicoptered to a nearby hospital where his physical wounds were successfully treated. (The psychological ones will probably remain for the rest of his life.)

A subsequent investigation by park rangers concluded that the bear that attacked Larson was most likely a female that had been traveling with a smaller bear, perhaps its cub, just prior to the incident. The larger bear was likely startled by

Larson's appearance and, grizzlies being highly territorial, it attacked what it viewed as a possibly hostile intruder.

Since there was no evidence that the bear had stalked Larson or otherwise displayed aberrant behavior, park officials decided to take no action against the animal.

In short, it was just being a grizzly bear.

IN THE SUMMER of 1996, Patricia Whiting-O'Keefe, her husband, Dr. Quinn O'Keefe, and Quinn's high-school friend Chad Hansen flew to Alaska for two weeks of backpacking near the Brooks Range. They were near Katak Lake, about 20 miles from the Lake Peters Research Station, when the men reportedly stopped to photograph arctic squirrels. Patricia, a Ph.D. in computer science, continued on about 100 yards over a slight rise and out of the men's line of sight. Turning around, she found herself in the path of a charging female grizzly bear, its single cub standing nearby.

"I saw her eyes focused on me and her mouth agape as her jaws closed over my head and face," Patricia later described in the January 1997 issue of *Outdoor Life* magazine. "I pushed up at her. I heard bone crunch. I perceived my flesh being torn away, but I didn't actually feel it at the time."

Like Ken Larson in the previous account, Patricia had the presence of mind to "play dead" even as the bear continued to swipe at her, inflicting several deep slashes across her leg and buttocks.

Hearing the attack, Quinn and Chad attempted to come to her aid, only to be chased away by yet a *second* female grizzly, this one traveling with *two* cubs.

When the bears finally departed, Quinn, a medical doctor, stayed with his critically injured wife as Chad sprinted the 20 miles to the Lake Peters Research Station on foot, a distance he covered in only five hours. Despite deteriorating weather conditions, a helicopter rescue mission was dispatched. Initially the helicopter pilot was unable to locate the O'Keefes—until Quinn managed to set fire to a wad of toilet paper he had with him and use its faint fire as a beacon. Patricia was then successfully airlifted to a hospital in Fairbanks, where she was attended by a physician experienced in treating animal-attack victims.

As a result of the incident, Patricia ended up losing her left eye and had to endure several elaborate skin grafts to repair her head wounds.

It's been speculated that the attack probably would not have occurred if Patricia had remained with her husband and friend. To date no bear has ever attacked three or more humans traveling close together. (A word to the wise to those who choose to hike alone.)

SOUTH COX, TWENTY-TWO, of Santa Rosa, California, was another individual who made the mistake of not only hiking alone but startling a mother bear with her cub. It was August 21, 1991, when the hardwood-floor finisher decided to go bow-hunting in the Marble Mountains Wilderness.

As reported in the August 28, 1991, *Los Angeles Times,* Cox happened upon a female black bear with two cubs and, since such animals are not legal game, decided to shoot them with a camera instead of his bow and arrow. He got within about 60 feet of the trio before clicking off his shoot. But the *snap* of the camera shutter apparently startled the mother bear, which charged the young man and attacked him ferociously, leaving him with 14 tooth-puncture wounds and numerous claw marks. Remarkably, he suffered no broken bones.

Cox later speculated that, since he was downwind and was wearing camouflaged clothing, the bear might have failed to recognize him as a human. He also noted that bears pop their teeth as a sign of aggression, a sound not unlike that of a clicking camera.

"She probably thought I was another bear and wanted to get me out of the way so I wouldn't harm her cubs," he speculated.

ALTHOUGH MANY BEAR attacks are clearly the acts of animals trying to protect their young, others are not so clearly explained. Such was the case of Juan Valle, an eight-year-old from Los Angeles's Watts neighborhood. Juan was delighted to have been chosen to participate in UCLA's UniCamp program, which for the past 60 years has given underprivileged children a chance to enjoy the peace and serenity of the great outdoors. But peace and serenity were exactly what young Juan *didn't* experience early on the morning of July 10, 1996, when his campsite was invaded by a yearling black bear believed to have weighed about 125 pounds.

The July 12, 1996, edition of the *Los Angeles Times* reported that the young bear wandered into the UniCamp site, located in a forested area near the city of La Crescenta, at approximately 5:30 A.M. and immediately went for the sleeping bags where Juan and several friends were still fast asleep. The bear reportedly took several swipes at Juan's head, twice gouging his scalp and just missing his left eyeball. Awoken by the screams of terrified children, counselors rushed to Juan's aid and managed to scare the bear away with shouts and wild gestures.

Juan was taken by ambulance to a nearby hospital where it took more than three hours for a doctor to stitch up his wounds, all of which were on the boy's head and face. Juan and the rest of the campers were sent home until the bear could be located and destroyed.

Game officials were at a loss to come up with a motive for the bear's unprovoked, violent behavior. As for Juan's reaction, "He was sad because he couldn't go back to camp," reported his twenty-year-old counselor, Showshan Yang.

JUAN VALLE WASN'T the only young camper whose enthusiasm for camping couldn't be dampened even by an encounter with a vicious bear. On the morning of August 7, 1993, twelve-year-old Boy Scout Bobby Clark of Los Angeles and his tentmate Brian Song were sleeping peacefully in a lean-to in the San Bernardino Mountains near Redlands when a 200-pound black bear came charging into their camp. According to a report in the August 8, 1993, *Los Angeles Times,* the alarmed counselors tried to scare the invader away by throwing rocks and shouting. But instead of retreating, the bear went for the lean-to and began swiping at Bobby's head.

"He woke me up," Bobby later recounted. "I kind of swatted at him and he basically started chewing on my head. It was pretty terrifying."

Ironically, another bear attack had occurred in the area just one week prior, and the Scout leaders had informed their charges of the importance of creating a "bear-safe camp," which involved, among other things, sleeping in groups.

Because of the attack, Bobby was forced to endure three and a half hours of surgery, including using a skin graft from his thigh to repair a wide 5-inch-long gouge in his scalp. A major facial nerve had been exposed but not severed, and as with the Juan Valle incident, Bobby's left eye just avoided being destroyed. Brian Song was also injured, requiring ten stitches in his arm.

Bobby received praise for his calm response to such a violent attack, and like Juan, he said he looked forward to returning to the woods.

"You've got to let your kids grow up and have experiences," Pam Clark, Bobby's mother, said. "You don't want things to happen to them, but by the same token you can't shelter them from everything."

"They were interested in a wilderness experience," Bob Clark, Bobby's father, added. "They got that in spades."

ALTHOUGH THE GRIZZLY bear is regarded as the most aggressive bear in North America, the polar bear is not far behind. A stunning example of the species' fierce behavior was reported in the December 2, 1993, *Los Angeles Times*. According to the account, crew members of the Oliktok Point radar base, a remote Air Force station situated on the Beaufort Sea northwest of Prudhoe Bay, had just finished dinner when a polar bear began pawing at the dining room window. The airmen tried to scare off the animal by banging on the window with a rolled-up magazine, but the beast's retreat was only momentary.

A few seconds later it hurled itself through the dining room window and began to chase fifty-five-year-old mechanic

Donald Chaffin into the adjacent recreation area, where it proceeded to maul him. Unable to verbally chase the bear away, the other airmen had no choice but to shoot the animal dead.

Why did the bear attack? It may have been drawn to the smell of food, or it might have just been curious.

"Polar bears do spend a good part of their lives breaking through ice getting at seals or other prey," noted federal biologist Scott Schliebe. "Breaking through a window wouldn't necessarily be real unusual behavior."

SURVIVING A BEAR ATTACK

Bear attacks are relatively rare, which is one of the reasons they're so dramatic. Since Glacier National Park opened to the public in 1910, bears have killed only nine people. Yellowstone, America's first and largest national park, has recorded only five deaths due to bears.

Still, attacks *do* happen. Here's what the experts suggest to improve your chances:

◎ **Travel in groups of three or more. Travel with an adult or older teenager whenever possible.**

◎ **Make loud noises while hiking. Most animals prefer to avoid human contact.**

◎ **If you see a bear, keep as far away from it as you can. Bears have been known to charge from distances of up to 150 yards.**

◎ **Many bears "bluff" charge, so if a bear does run toward you, stand your ground. Wave your arms to appear larger than you really are. Wait for the bear to stop, then slowly back away.**

◎ **If the bear keeps coming, hit the ground and play dead. There's one exception to this rule. If you believe the bear has been stalking you prior to the attack, then chances are it sees you not as a threat but as food. In this case, scream and fight like hell.**

◎ **Older teens and adults might want to carry a can of pepper spray. It has been effective in turning back some bears, especially smaller ones.**

chapter 2

Top Cats

Call it a cougar, a puma, or a mountain lion. Whichever name you prefer, we're talking about one of the most aggressive and prevalent predators on the North American continent. Although the large, graceful cats were once found everywhere from Southern British Columbia to South America, widespread hunting over the last two centuries brought the animals close to extinction. Today they're found principally in wilderness areas, particularly on the West Coast of the United States.

Male mountain lion can grow up to 7 feet from snout to tail. Although the cats eat a variety of foods, they're known to prefer meat, particularly deer. Like most wild animals, they tend to avoid human contact, but with cities expanding further and further into what were once undeveloped hills and mountain ranges, encounters between humans and mountain lions are becoming more frequent.

Most of the mountain lions residing in the United States can be found in California, which outlawed hunting the animals back in 1972, allowing their once-diminishing numbers to grow substantially. Game officials estimate their numbers now range from 5,500 to nearly 10,000 in California alone. Protecting the animals has proven to be a double-edged sword. Between 1909 and 1985 there were no reported attacks on humans by the big cats. Then, in 1986, two people were attacked. There have been seven more attacks since 1992, and their numbers are expected to keep growing along with the mountain lion population.

Here are just some of the most recent episodes.

TROY AND ROBIN Winslow of Sebastopol, California, accompanied by their friends Charles and Kathleen Strehl of Eureka, as well as their pet collie, had gone up to a cabin in the hills of Mendocino County north of San Francisco for a vacation. On the morning of August 16, 1994, at approximately 4:30 A.M., the four were awakened by frantic barking from the dog, which had been tied up outside. Looking out the window they were horrified to see the collie locked in mortal combat with a mountain lion.

The *San Jose Mercury News* reported that when the couples finally got outside with a flashlight, they found that the dog was gone and that the big cat had curled itself up beneath the cabin.

The Winslows and Strehls built an outdoor fire to help ward off the 40-degree predawn cold and waited for the mountain lion to emerge. Indeed, it showed itself about thirty minutes later and lunged straight for Kathleen Strehl, biting her in the left forearm. Using the only weapons they had available, a knife and shovel, the other three then attacked the snarling beast until they had beaten it to death.

Troy Winslow lost his thumb in the attack. The collie that had warned them of the cougar was later found injured, but miraculously alive, with multiple bites on its face.

It took the couples two hours to drive to the hospital, where they were treated for their injuries. The dog was treated by a local veterinarian.

Local game officials could determine no reason for the attack, other than perhaps the cougar saw the collie as an invader of its territory.

ON THE AFTERNOON of March 20, 1995, twenty-seven-year-old Scott Fike was bicycling alone along a trail in the San Gabriel Mountains above the city of Altadena, northeast of Los Angeles, when a large female mountain lion weighing close to 100 pounds suddenly leaped out of the underbrush and began loping alongside him. Fike immediately got off his bike and ran down into a canyon, hoping to evade the animal, but it pursued and attacked him when he slipped and fell to the ground.

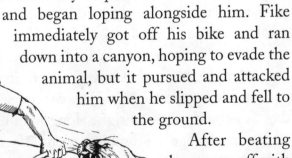

After beating the cougar off with his bare hands, Fike was able to chase it off by throwing rocks at it. Fike immediately reported the attack to game officials, who used dogs to track it down. The cougar was found at the bottom of the canyon eating a deer carcass. It was chased for several hundred yards, then dispatched with a single shot to the head.

The *Los Angeles Times* covered the attack and ensuing chase in their March 26, 1995, edition. In it, State Fish and Game Warden Mark Jeter noted that the attack appeared to be totally unprovoked. Although the cat was a female, it did not appear to have been nursing, and there were no cubs found in the area. "The weird part was . . . he [Fike] fought it off aggressively as he's supposed to, and he was still attacked," Jeter stated.

SUSAN GROVES, TWENTY-FIVE, is a water-quality specialist who, on the afternoon of December 14, 1994, was collecting samples at a stream feeding Colorado's Animas-LaPlata water project when she heard something moving along the riverbank above her. At first she ignored the sounds, but when they persisted, she turned and found herself staring into the eyes of a golden cougar.

"As soon as we made eye contact, it came down the embankment to me," Groves stated in an article carried nationwide by the *Chicago Tribune* wire service the following day. "The lion followed right along with me, and as I crossed under the bridge I stumbled, went down in the icy water, filling both of my waders. That's when it sunk its teeth in my head and held me under."

Groves struggled violently even as the big cat tried to drown her. Somehow she wound up on the riverbank with her arm still in the cougar's mouth.

"Then I reached into my fishing vest, found a pair of forceps and started jabbing the lion in the eyes with them," she stated. The lion retreated and Susan struggled to her feet, wobbled back to where her truck was parked, and drove off looking for assistance.

Although the mountain lion was later caught and destroyed, authorities could find no reason for the attack. It was just one more example of nature being chillingly and violently unpredictable.

WHAT TO DO WHEN YOU SEE A MOUNTAIN LION

Because they're a protected species in many states, mountain lions are becoming more and more populous in the western United States. Here are some tips wildlife experts offer on how to minimize your chances of being attacked by one of these magnificent but often aggressive predators:

- ◎ When hiking or biking in wilderness areas, always travel in groups.

- ◎ Parents should closely supervise their children. The smaller the individual, the more likely a mountain lion is to see him or her as prey.

- ◎ When you see a mountain lion, stand your ground, then slowly back away, always maintaining eye contact. Never approach a cougar or, on the other extreme, run away. If a child is with you, pick him or her up but don't bend down while doing so.

- ◎ Don't scream. This may startle a mountain lion or make it think you're wounded and therefore an easier target.

- ◎ Do whatever you can to make yourself look larger. Wave your arms slowly over your head or open your jacket to give yourself the illusion of greater size.

- ◎ Unlike with bears, if a mountain lion attacks, you don't play dead. Instead, fight back. Use anything at your disposal, such as rocks, branches, your camera, etc.

chapter  3

Raging Rattlers

The rattlesnake, along with buffalo, gold mines, and saguaro cacti, is one of the great icons of the American West. Members of the Viperidae family, which also includes copperheads and cottonmouths, rattlesnakes are distinguished by their tail rattles, which serve to alert potential attackers, as well as their flat heads and large fangs that fold inward and lie horizontally when their mouths are closed. The most common variety found in California is the Pacific rattler, which can grow up to 6 feet long.

Rattlesnakes can be found throughout the West, particularly in wilderness areas but also on hillsides and in outlying suburbs. "Rattlesnake season" is generally regarded to

WHEN YOU'RE BIT BY A RATTLER

You've probably seen this scene in a hundred different Westerns: A cowboy is bitten by a rattlesnake. The first thing his buddy does is tie the wounded appendage off with a tourniquet. Then, after giving the victim a shot of whiskey to help dull the pain, he cuts the wound open with a knife and sucks out the poison.

That's Hollywood. In real life, here's how you should *really* handle a snakebite, according to the experts:

◎ **Don't touch the wound. Take the victim to the nearest emergency room.**

◎ **Remove watches, bracelets, rings, and other constricting jewelry from the victim—hands, arms, and legs tend to swell after a snakebite.**

◎ **Don't cut or suck the wound.**

◎ **Don't apply a tourniquet.**

◎ **Don't pack the wound in ice.**

◎ **Don't give the victim any alcohol.**

occur between the months of April and October, when the weather is warm and the snakes come out to sun themselves. Heavy rains and floods can also drive them out of their burrows into areas where they're more likely to come into human contact. Every year local fire departments and animal control agencies respond to literally thousands of rattlesnake reports throughout the Southwest.

The rattlesnake's principal diet is rodents, so attacks on humans usually occur only in self-defense. Most bites occur when a snake is stepped on, cornered, or—in far too many cases—actually picked up.

Rattlesnake venom is hemorrhagic, meaning it destroys tissue. Usually the damage is confined to the area of the bite, but if the venom gets into the bloodstream, it can cause damage throughout the body. In a normal, healthy adult, a rattler bite usually won't prove fatal, although it can leave a person sick for weeks. However, the victim's sensitivity to venom, as well as the size of the snake, can play a role in how severe the reaction will be. (Usually, the bigger the snake, the more venom it releases.) Fortunately for humans, a good portion of rattlesnake bites are "dry bites," meaning no venom is released.

Reports of rattlesnake attacks occur regularly in the West. Some even prove fatal. Here are some recent occurrences.

DURING A ONE-WEEK period in early May 1992, five people were reported bitten by rattlesnakes in Northern California. The one fatality was Daniel Pearls, twenty, of Lake County.

Because Pearls was alone at the time of the attack, the specifics of the incident can never be known for sure. However, details contained in a story carried by the Associated Press on May 12, 1992, suggest one likely scenario.

It appears that Pearls was alone fishing on the shores of a local lake when he saw a small snake on the ground nearby. Curious, he picked up the snake and held it close to his face to get a closer look. It was clearly a baby. It was also a rattlesnake. Startled, the rattler lunged forward and bit Pearls on the lip. Although the snake was small, the bite proved fatal—Pearls died before he could receive help.

JULIA JIMENEZ, FIFTY-THREE, of East San Jose, California, had been visiting Alum Rock Park ever since she was a child. Now a grandmother, she saw nothing wrong with taking two of her grandchildren, Ruben Tapia, seven, and James Moisa, eleven, to the park for a few hours of healthy outdoor recreation.

According to a report carried in the June 18, 1997, edition of the *San Jose Mercury News*, Ruben had been well trained by his uncle to look out for snakes and mountain lions when in the wilderness areas. However, when he wandered off about 50 yards from the park's main playground area, he encountered a snake that bit him. Immediately rushing to her screaming grandson's aid, Jimenez dispatched James to confirm that the snake was, in fact, a rattler. He returned with a description of a snake approximately 12 inches long with four rattlers on its tail.

Ruben was rushed to Valley Medical Center where doctors verified that the bite was poisonous and administered antivenin. This was the first reported snakebite to occur at the facility in five years.

SECTION 2

WATER WARS

Terror from Beneath the Waves

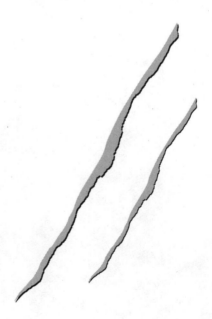

chapter 4

Shark!

Although the concept of a "man-eating" shark has been around for about as long as humans have ventured into the water, it was Steven Spielberg's 1975 megahit *Jaws,* based on the best-selling Peter Benchley novel, that seared the image of the nearly mythic underwater killer into the imaginations of people worldwide. There are few of us who can see a triangular fin slicing through the waves without hearing the film's sinister "DUM-DUM-DUM-DUM" theme in our minds or imagining the blood-spurting carnage so dramatically captured in that immortal thriller.

Sharks *can* be every bit as deadly—although perhaps not quite as large, intelligent, or persistent—as the one featured in *Jaws.* With ancestors dating back 300 million years, sharks are elegantly simple creatures whose torpedo-shaped bodies and multiple rows of serrated teeth make them some of the sea's most efficient predators.

Of the approximately 250 known shark species, the vast majority are relatively harmless. Some, such as the thresher, brown, and lemon shark, are even commercially fished for food. However, the black-tipped shark, which usually grows from 3 to 4 feet long, and the dreaded great white, which can reach lengths of over 20 feet, are quite aggressive. In fact, the great white regularly preys on marine mammals such as sea lions, otters, and even dolphins—animals other sharks choose to ignore.

In North America, most shark attacks occur along the East Coast, with the smaller black-tipped sharks usually responsible. Florida, with its warmer waters, is a favorite hunting ground for these predatory fishes, although Georgia and Texas have also had a number of attacks as well. Along the West Coast, shark attacks are usually confined to California, and here it's the infamous great white that's almost always the culprit. In Hawaii, where attacks on swimmers and surfers occur in relatively small numbers, tiger sharks are usually to blame.

Although some shark attacks are fatal, most are not. Many marine biologists have speculated on why sharks attack humans and then often retreat. The consensus suggests that sharks, being pretty dim-witted, initially mistake humans for more familiar prey, such as fishes or sea lions, and go for the kill. However, once they get a taste of a person, they're disappointed by the low fat content, as well as intimidated by humans' relatively large size. (Most marine mammals, especially seals and sea lions, have fatty flesh, which sharks are believed to find much more flavorful than a human's.)

All of which is little consolation for those people who have lost flesh, limbs, and even their lives to these powerful predators of the deep.

Bill Kennedy of Ventura County, California, had seen the movie *Jaws* a year before going surfing off Moonstone Beach in Northern California's Humboldt County. Kennedy was twenty-five years old when, just after noon on October 18, 1976, he paddled out into the saves, the ominous "DUM-DUM-DUM-DUM" theme throbbing in his head.

Twenty years later he related his harrowing experience in a story that appeared in the October 20, 1996, issue of the *Los Angeles Times*. He described seeing a flock of about a hundred ducks suddenly take to the air, and could feel danger closing in around him.

"I got a premonition that I should follow my instinct and get out of the water," Kennedy said. "But I didn't follow my instinct."

According to the report, Kennedy was laying on his surfboard when a 10-foot-long great white shark attacked him from behind. The fish grabbed one leg in its awesome jaws, but the force of the impact tilted both Kennedy and his board upward at a 20-degree angle, causing him to slide free of the predator's grasp.

Terrified but not yet in any pain, Kennedy reportedly caught the next wave and headed straight for shore. It was there that he saw a huge gash in his leg, one that would eventually require 35 stitches.

Eight years after the attack, Kennedy met Carolyn Hanson, an aspiring screenwriter, at a local gym. Although Carolyn was at first shocked and sickened by the massive scars on Kennedy's leg, they still managed to fall in love and get married. She now describes her husband's ordeal as "an incredible story"—like one right out of the movies! Now he looks back on that experience as the scariest of his life.

IN EARLY SEPTEMBER 1995, thirty-year-old Bryan Hillenburg, who is deaf, was abalone diving with his roommate, thirty-two-year-old Michael Burns, in an area known as Shelter Cove, located approximately 150 miles north of San Francisco. According to reports carried by both the *Los Angeles Times* and the *Long Beach Press Telegram*, Hillenburg, a resident of San Jose, had just surfaced and was putting abalone into a diving bag on his kayak when a shark, presumably a great white, clamped onto his left leg.

Burns immediately saw what was going on and helped pull Hillenburg from the shark's mouth. He then alerted three other divers in the area, who helped bring them both ashore.

Hillenburg ultimately underwent three and a half hours of surgery. Fifty staples were required to close the huge wound. In addition, four shark's teeth were removed from his leg, including one that had gotten lodged into his leg bone.

"It's like an obsession," Hillenburg later told the Associated Press in a typed computer interview. "I see it so clearly. It just repeats over and over."

IN ONE OF the few actual deaths attributed to great whites in recent years, a forty-year-old Santa Barbara man (name withheld) was killed on December 9, 1994, while diving for urchins near San Miguel Island, part of California's Channel Islands. According to an Associated Press story issued the next day, two men aboard the 34-foot fishing boat *Florentina Marie* pulled the wounded diver aboard and found a massive gash on his right leg. They called for a Coast Guard helicopter rescue and began performing CPR. But the diver stopped breathing, and by the time he arrived at the hospital 90 minutes later, he was already dead.

Experts deduced that the attacker was a great white due to the nature of the wound and the fact that female great whites are known to breed around the Channel Islands during late autumn.

chapter 5

Galloping Gators

esidents of Southern Florida have more than just a casual acquaintance with the *Alligator mississipiensis,* otherwise known as the American alligator. Like the California cougar, the Florida gator was nearly hunted to extinction during the first half of the twentieth century, before it was declared an endangered species, and has since come back with a vengeance. Today, game and wildlife officials estimate that there are more than 1 million alligators in Florida alone, living in the state's 6.7 million acres of swamp as well as thousands of freshwater pockets in and around outlying residential areas. Florida's large network of canals and underground waterways has proven to be a superhighway system for the big reptiles, allowing them to move about and breed with amazing speed.

Alligators usually grow to lengths of 6 to 8 feet, although 20-footers are not unknown. Nocturnal creatures, they tend to rest during daylight hours, although they've been known to have a midday snack should one become available.

With the human population moving ever outward from established urban centers, encounters with alligators have become more common. Each year Florida authorities respond to more than 6,000 "nuisance alligator" calls and destroy about 3,000 of the animals that have encroached into human space.

More often than not, alligators will go after small prey, such as chickens and household pets. But attacks on humans occur with uncomfortable frequency. In fact, since 1943, the first year Florida's Game and Fresh Water Fish Commission began keeping records, there have been 225 attacks on people, eight of which proved fatal.

Here are just a few stories that were recently reported.

THE DISAPPEARANCE OF three-year-old Adam Trevor Binford on March 19, 1997, made national news. According to reports carried by the Associated Press, *Miami Herald,* and *Orlando Sentinel,* the boy had been wading knee-deep off the shores of Lake Ashby, a 3,200-acre body of water situated between Daytona Beach and Orlando, picking water lilies for his mother when the attack occurred. His mother, Lorri Ann Binford, thirty-one, a waitress from New Smyrna Beach; his brother, Evan, eight; his cousin Cassidy Bass, nine; and the family dog, Charley, were all nearby.

According to the reports, Lorri Ann had turned away when she heard a loud *splash,* one that was "too loud" to have been made by the boy simply falling into the water. When she turned around, the boy was already gone.

Lorri Ann called authorities right away, speculating that an alligator had snatched her boy. Wildlife officials immediately began searching the lake, but it wasn't until the next day that a state-licensed trapper found the suspect alligator about a mile from the abduction site. The 11-foot, 450-pound male reportedly still had the boy's torso clutched in its teeth, and one of the victim's arms was missing. The animal was killed on the spot.

Game and Fresh Water Fish Commission investigators speculated that the alligator had been stalking Adam's dog, Charley, prior to attacking the boy himself.

As for Adam, experts believe his death was swift and virtually painless.

"There's no question [Adam] died almost immediately," said Jim Downing, medical examiner assistant in Volusia County, as reported in the March 25, 1997, *Miami Herald.* "He never knew what hit him. The minute they grab their prey, they submerge and roll. The extreme amount of trauma is too much."

THE TEIXERIA FAMILY of Brazil was on vacation in the Florida Everglades when they acquired an unexpected—and unwanted—souvenir. On the afternoon of July 13, 1996, the family was bicycling along the popular Tamiami Trail when seven-year-old Alexandre fell off his bike into shallow water and was immediately set upon by a 5- to 6-foot alligator, which clamped onto the boy's chest.

According to a report in the July 16, 1996, *Miami Herald,* Alexandre received puncture wounds to his left shoulder and arm, as well as his left lung. The boy's parents immediately rushed to his aid. Mrs. Teixeria swiped her arm at the reptile and received a bite wound of her own as a result.

Alexandre was eventually pulled free of the gator's jaws and taken immediately to a Miami hospital, where both he and his mother were treated for their injuries. Alexandre had to be held for several days while blood was drained from his damaged lung. The family returned to Brazil shortly after his release with a story none of them is likely to ever forget.

EVENINGS IN SOUTHERN Florida can be awfully hot, even in late September, so ten-year-old Timothy Blake Langdon and his friends decided to cool off with a late afternoon swim in Ocean Pond, a 1,700-acre lake near Olustee. It was about 5 P.M. on Saturday, September 23, 1995, when the boys' reverie was shattered by the sudden appearance of an 8-foot-long alligator, which suddenly grabbed the fifth-grader and dragged him underwater.

The gator emerged a few seconds later and, to the surprise of many, released the boy. Timothy was immediately taken ashore and rushed to the hospital where he was treated for an inch-long gash on the right side of his chest as well as numerous bite wounds to his chest and back.

In a report carried in the *Miami Herald* two days later, Game and Fresh Water Fish Commission spokesman Dewey Weaver suggested why the attack had been so brief. "The fact that the boy was only taken under once and then released tends to make us believe it was a reaction to being surprised rather than a hunt for food," he stated.

Which was good news for Timothy but still bad news for the alligator, which was ultimately hunted down and destroyed.

WOULD A PERSON *willingly* throw him- or herself into a lake full of alligators? That was the question raised by the curious death of Virginia Grace Eberhart, who lived in a Miami-area trailer park with her husband, a retired Marine Corps sergeant suffering from Alzheimer's disease.

According to the October 6, 1993, *Miami Herald,* the seventy-year-old Eberhart had been suffering from terminal cancer and was down to a mere 80 pounds on the night of the incident. Heavily medicated, she had apparently gone for a walk sometime after 10:30 P.M. on Saturday, October 2. Either inadvertently or on purpose, she ended up tumbling down a 15-foot slope into the waters of Lake Serenity, a 4-acre pond on the edge of the trailer park. There, a 9- to 10-foot-long alligator grabbed her head and snapped her neck, killing her instantly.

A neighbor, Jack Horrocks, sixty-nine, was the first to spot her body the next morning. Looking out his trailer window through binoculars, he saw an alligator on shore holding what he first thought was the body of a large bird.

"I looked out and saw this big, big gator flipping this body up in the air," Horrocks said. "It was horrible."

There was some speculation that Eberhart, no longer able to live with her pain, had willingly thrown herself into the pond. But many doubt this theory.

"She didn't commit suicide," stated neighbor Frank E. Champagne. "She was a very religious Catholic. And what woman would commit suicide by going into a lake full of alligators in the dark?"

Trappers later killed more than a half dozen alligators that had taken up residence in Lake Serenity. Eberhart's left arm was found in the belly of one of them. Her right arm was never recovered.

NOTHING CAN BE more terrifying than seeing your own child killed before your very eyes. But such was the horror experienced by Gary Weidenhamer of Lantana, Florida, on June 19, 1993.

Weidenhamer and his wife, Donna, were accompanying their ten-year-old son, Bradley, and several members of his Little League team, the Lantana Minor League Tigers, on a canoe trip along the Loxahatchee River in Jonathan Dickinson State Park. They were surrounded by more than a dozen other canoes when the group of canoers all stepped out to carry their boats over some fallen tree limbs.

"I heard someone say, 'A gator has taken somebody,' " Weidenhamer said in a June 21, 1993, *Miami Herald* interview. "I called for my son and I realized he was missing. Then I saw something white in the water. I went and grabbed the white spot. I pulled. I got him up enough to see it was Bradley."

The alligator, estimated to be between 11 and 12 feet long, had grabbed the 10-year-old by the head. It dove underwater even as Weidenhamer tried frantically to pull his son free. Other boaters gathered around and began beating the reptile with their oars.

The alligator finally released the boy, and his father immediately began giving him CPR. While the alligator continued to look on from just a few yards away, Weidenhamer and other parents then put the boy in a canoe and paddled him to a tourist stopping point about a mile away where they called for help. A rescue helicopter arrived soon after and flew the victim to a local hospital, but his injuries were too severe.

"Even if the Traumahawk [rescue helicopter] had landed right then and gotten to him, I don't think they could have helped," Weidenhamer stated.

Ironically, this same alligator had reportedly been targeted several weeks earlier for removal when reports of its so-called "friendly" behavior became known to the Florida Game and Fresh Water Fish Commission. The gator purportedly had exhibited behavior that indicated it had been fed by humans and thus had lost its fear of people. However, no action was taken against the animal at the time, and there remains some debate as to whether or not this was, in fact, the same gator that killed Bradley Weidenhamer.

EVEN ONE OF America's most popular tourist meccas is not totally free of alligator infestation. On Friday, October 10, 1986, three children were playing tetherball at Walt Disney World's Fort Wilderness campground when a decidedly non-animatronic alligator made an unwelcome appearance. According to a report carried on the *Miami Herald's* national wire service on October 13, 1986, Paul Richard Santamaria, eight, of Bristol, New Hampshire, wandered from the play area to watch ducks waddling around a small pond several yards away.

As he stood at the water's edge, a 7-foot, 4-inch female gator suddenly lunged out of the water and bit the terrified third-grader in the left leg, leaving several deep scratches and puncture wounds in his thigh, knee, and lower leg.

His sister, Carolyn, twelve, reportedly ran over and grabbed her brother under the arms and pulled. At the same time his brother, Joseph Jr., ten, ran over and began to beat the alligator's head with his bare hands. At that point the reptile released the boy and returned to the pond. Paul spent the weekend at the hospital, where his wounds were treated. Fortunately, none of them was deemed serious.

A spokesman for the Walt Disney Company said that this was the first attack he was aware of at the campground. "We have a program for moving them when they are in an area where guests are," spokesman Bob Mervine stated. "But obviously, we didn't move enough."

DON'T FEED THE GATORS!

Alligators are as much a part of Florida living as mosquitoes, armadillos, and flying cockroaches. And far too often people—both tourists and local alike—make the mistake of treating these animals like exotic pets. This is especially true of smaller alligators, whose diminutive size make them appear relatively harmless.

State wildlife officials warn people who encounter alligators, whether in the wild or in outlying urban areas, to keep a safe distance, and *never* to try to feed them. Alligators, like virtually all animals, are naturally afraid of people, but when they start to associate humans with a good meal, the results can be fatal.

chapter **6**

Some More "Fish Stories"

harks and alligators are perhaps the two most celebrated of nature's water-dwelling predators. However, on occasion, reports surface of other attacks by less notable, but still decidedly nasty, denizens of the deep.

Here are just a few that have been reported in the national media over the past few years.

ON AUGUST 7, 1993, Neal Conan, host of National Public Radio's "Weekend Edition," interviewed Scharf Turner, a fishing boat captain operating out of St. Petersburg, Florida. According to Capt. Turner, he, his son, and a few friends were out fishing when one of his guests, Tina Depui, indicated that she had hooked a small fish.

What happened next was one of the great fish stories of the decade. As detailed by Capt. Turner, the fish, a barracuda measuring 51 inches long and weighing about 30 pounds, actually *leaped* into the boat, just missing Depui's head. It slammed onto the deck and began thrashing about, smashing the engine's ignition switch, which effectively disabled the vessel.

Capt. Turner grabbed an aluminum baseball bat and began beating the barracuda, which continued to lash out with its powerful tail and long, tooth-filled mouth.

"For about five minutes, it was kind of touch and go," Capt. Turner told Conan. "We weren't sure who was going to win." It look him five entire minutes to finally kill the fish.

Turner dismissed any notion that the barracuda was actually targeting someone on the boat. "I think that it's an instinct for the fish to react when it feels that it is either hooked or there is something unnatural happening to whatever it has in its mouth, and it is an instinct to jump. The fact that it jumped into a boat . . . Well, it could have jumped in 359 other directions, you know," he stated.

Depui later took the barracuda's jaws back home to California as a souvenir.

USA Today REPORTED in its June 5, 1997, issue that Mary Anne Boyer, thirty-one, of Miami, Florida, had been attacked by a barracuda while fishing the previous day. The fish reportedly injured a good portion of her left arm, permanently leaving her without the use of her left hand.

IN OCTOBER 1994, Lynne Cox, an endurance swimmer from Los Alamitos, California, decided to make a two-day-long "peace swim" across the Gulf of Aqaba between Egypt's Sinai Peninsula and Saudi Arabia to support reconciliation between Israel, Egypt, and Jordan, all three of which border the gulf. The swim not only resulted in an invitation to personally attend the signing of the Israel/Jordan peace treaty, but also 35 painful jellyfish stings that she suffered along her route.

AS REPORTED IN the December 23, 1996, issue of *USA Today*, Christmastime tourists found their vacation plans disrupted when, on December 21, 1996, swimmers in the waters off Hawaii's Ala Moana and Waikiki beaches found themselves facing an invasion of the large, toxic jellyfish known as the Portuguese man-of-war. Approximately 40 people were treated in local hospitals for the painful, sometimes deadly stings.

Adams County Dist. 12
North Star Elementary School
8740 North Star Dr.
Thornton, CO 80260-4322

SECTION 3

CREEPY CRAWLERS

Small But Deadly

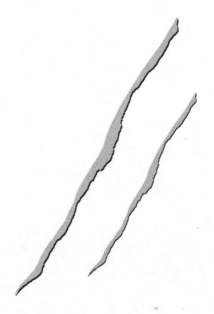

chapter 7

Itsy-Bitsy Spiders

rachnophobia is more than just the name of a 1990 horror movie. It's a genuine fear of spiders that affects millions of people worldwide. Many otherwise fearless individuals—policemen, soldiers, skydivers, mountain climbers—become quivering bowls of Jell-O when confronted with an arachnid.

The truth is, most spiders are on *our* side. They spend most of their time eating insect pests we'd just as soon do

without. And although many common species can inflict irritating, sometimes painful bites, only four of the world's known 34,000 species actually carry venom capable of killing an adult human. Of these, only two, the black widow and the brown recluse, are found in North America.

(A fifth species, the wolf spider, which is a fast, hairy spider about the size of a hockey puck, is responsible for numerous injuries, not because of anything it does but because of what panicked *people* do to get away from one.)

Both black widows and brown recluses are shy, nonaggressive creatures that usually won't bite unless disturbed. The black widow—so named because the female eats the male shortly after mating—is black, about the size of a blueberry, and easily recognized by the red hourglass-shaped marking on the underside of its abdomen. The brown recluse—which likes to hide in dark, dry places, including people's shoes—is a thin, spindly creature also known as the fiddler spider or violin spider because of the violinlike marking on the front portion of its body.

All spider bites contain two puncture holes from the fangs, which the spider uses to insert venom into its intended prey. Black widow bites produce virulent, flulike symptoms, which can include muscle aches and fever that can last for days. Brown recluse bites usually result in painful, burning feelings as well as large ulcers that, if left untreated, can result in serious tissue damage.

Although infinitely more common than attacks by grizzly bears, sharks, alligators, and other large predators, encounters with spiders do occasionally make the news—especially when the victims experience serious, even fatal reactions.

It happens more often than you might think.

IN JULY 1992, Valerie Slimp, forty, of Mira Loma, California, was shampooing her carpet when she felt what she later described as a sharp pain in her right thigh. At first she thought that she had merely pulled a muscle, but the pain increased, and she began to experience headaches, muscle pains, and nausea. Two days later she fell into a coma.

According to several stories by the Associated Press, which covered the woman's ordeal for nearly a year, Slimp awoke five months later to discover that both her arms, her legs, and tissue from her nose had been amputated. She was told that she had been bitten by a poisonous spider—most likely a brown recluse—and that the amputations were done to stop advancing blood poisoning.

Married with two children, Slimp has since been fitted with artificial limbs and requires an electric wheelchair to move about.

"I always thought if anything was going to happen it would be a car accident or something," she told the Associated Press in a story published on May 23, 1993. "Maybe get hit by a Mack truck you don't see coming. But to get bit by a spider?"

The Slimp case is one of the most dramatic cases of spider bite reactions reported in the past decade.

WHEN ARE PEOPLE more vulnerable than when they're on the toilet? That's exactly where Robert Edington, a thirty-three-year-old construction foreman from Margate, Florida, was when he had his nearly fatal encounter with a black widow spider. The September 30, 1989, *Miami Herald* reported that a week earlier, Edington had been working at a building site in the city of Delray Beach when he excused himself to use a portable toilet. While sitting on the toilet, he felt a stinging sensation between his thighs.

"My whole body started getting numb, from my knees up to my stomach," Edington said. "It started getting all numb and really hurting, real bad."

When Edington arrived at a nearby hospital, the doctors at first thought the man was suffering from kidney stones or appendicitis. It wasn't until later that Edington even mentioned being bitten. Antivenin was administered, and two days of hospitalization followed. Edington lost 18 pounds during his prolonged recovery.

"I was screaming, yelling, and begging for someone to help me, praying to God," Edington related. "If I ever had to go through this pain again, if I knew it couldn't be cured, I would want them to kill me."

CIRCUIT JUDGE MARK Speiser of Broward County, Florida, thought he'd heard every excuse in the book for failed court appearances. But on September 13, 1993, he got a new one: The probation officer for Linda Beavers, who was due to surrender herself for a probation violation stemming from a drunk-driving arrest a year and a half earlier, said that the woman would not be able to appear due to a spider bite. And not just *any* kind of spider bite. It was the bite of a brown recluse.

After hearing the details of the case and a description of the debilitating nature of such bites, Judge Speiser agreed to reschedule the hearing for the following week.

"Sitting as a judge, hearing excuses becomes commonplace," Judge Speiser told the *Miami Herald* in an interview the next day. "But hearing the spider excuse expands the web of explanations. If it's true, my heart goes out to her."

POLICE FROM BOSTON'S tough Roxbury precincts face danger on a daily basis. But nothing could have prepared Sergeants Patrick Cullity and Loman McClinton Jr. for the life-and-death struggle they were to endure while on duty during March 1994.

According to a story carried in the May 18, 1994, *Boston Globe,* it began when Sgt. Cullity, who was working the night shift, pulled some reports from a file cabinet. Several minutes later he felt his feet beginning to swell and tingle. Thinking his shoes were merely too tight, he loosened his laces, but that provided no relief. Soon he became dizzy, his mouth became dry, and his foot pain became unbearable. Experiencing chills and fever, he went to a nearby hospital, where doctors, thinking he merely had the flu, sent him home with antibiotics.

But the symptoms persisted for a full week, by which time Sgt. Cullity's right foot had turned black and purple and felt "like it was going to explode." He finally sought the help of a specialist, who diagnosed the problem as a recluse spider bite. The doctor reportedly told Cullity that if he had waited much longer, the infection could have spread to his bone, resulting in an amputation.

Apparently Cullity's area commander, Deputy Super-intendent Bobbie Johnson, was first skeptical that her veteran sergeant had, in fact, been felled by a simple insect.

But when Sgt. McClinton, who also worked the night shift at Roxbury, checked himself into the hospital after complaining of stinging on his back, exterminators were called in to check the station house. What they found was a ³/₈-inch-long brown recluse that had made its nest, complete with eggs and babies, on the second floor behind one of the station's file cabinets. The building was shut down for fumigation, and a temporary mobile command post was set up in the parking lot so that community services could be maintained.

As for Sergeants Cullity and McClinton, they've learned firsthand that bad guys don't always walk on just two legs.

EVEN GREAT MEN can fall victim to the lowly spider. In September 1988, press reports nationwide carried news of evangelist Billy Graham's hospitalization for what was at first believed to be a simple foot infection. As it turned out, this spiritual adviser to presidents had been bitten by a brown recluse spider.

In a report carried by the *Mercury News* wire service on September 7, 1988, A. Larry Ross, a spokesman for Graham, noted that the evangelist was bitten earlier in the week while at his home in North Carolina's Appalachian Mountains. He sought help from a local doctor, who properly diagnosed the bite as that of a brown recluse, but no further action was taken. Graham's symptoms grew worse until, while in New York for a weeklong crusade, he was forced to check himself into a hospital in Rochester. After two days of treatment, Graham was released and allowed to continue his crusade—with perhaps even more than his usual respect for the power of God's handiwork.

TIPS FOR ARACHNOPHOBES

◎ To avoid spider bites, always wear heavy gloves when doing yardwork or when cleaning out garages and/or attics. Black widows and brown recluses are rarely found in homes, but they love to make their nests in quiet, out-of-the-way places like woodpiles and storage sheds.

◎ If you are bitten, clean the area immediately with soap and water to remove as much venom as possible.

◎ If swelling occurs, put ice on the wound.

◎ If the area becomes unusually sore or flulike symptoms develop, go straight to your local emergency room. Quick treatment is the best way to avoid a long, painful recovery.

◎ If you can kill the offending arachnid, do so and keep it for later identification. Knowing what species bit you can go a long way to designing a proper course of treatment.

chapter

Scorpio Rising

Like spiders, scorpions are arachnids whose very form inspires dread in many people. But unlike poisonous spiders, scorpions are not found in most areas of the United States, preferring only the hot, dry climate of the desert Southwest.

Scorpions can grow anywhere from ½-inch to 7 inches long and immobilize their prey by a sting from their characteristic high, curved tails. Most of the species found in the United States are incapable of killing an adult human being, although there are some Mexican varieties whose venom has proved fatal.

Although scorpion stings are fairly common to people who live in Arizona and New Mexico, few are dramatic enough to make news. But every once in a while, an unusual and chilling encounter does occur.

ON FEBRUARY 26, 1996, San Francisco Giants shortstop Shawon Dunston was reportedly stretching with his teammates in the Indian School Park gym when a scorpion crawled unseen onto his shoulder. Before he knew what was happening, he was stung twice near the base of his neck.

"It was a little scary," Dunston said in an interview printed the next day in the *San Jose Mercury News*.

"We put the sneak attack on [the scorpion]," second baseman Robby Thompson added. Thompson and rehabilitation coordinator Stan Conte located the scorpion and swatted it before it could make its escape.

Dunston reportedly felt no pain until ice was applied to the affected area. He was then taken to a local hospital, where he was given a tetanus shot. Except for some residual soreness, the sting had no serious aftereffects.

THE SCENARIO EXPERIENCED by thirteen-month-old Anders Bjella of Costa Mesa, California, was not nearly as benign as the shortstop's. As related in several stories carried in the *Los Angeles Times* in December 1994, young Anders accompanied his parents on a Christmastime vacation to Puerto Vallarta, Mexico. Although the parents had been "casually warned about scorpions," they didn't bother checking their son's shoes before putting them on his feet for a walk into town.

"He jumped off the bed and took a few steps and yelped," mother Diane Bjella said. "We thought he hit his mouth . . . he's getting new teeth."

As they walked into town, the child reportedly began crying uncontrollably. His lips turned purple and he began frothing at the mouth. They quickly returned to their villa, removed the boy's shoes, and only then saw a large scorpion skitter out.

Seeing that their son had been stung numerous times, they immediately rushed Anders to a local hospital, but the doctors there saw little hope for the boy's recovery. He was already running a temperature of 104 and would frequently stop breathing.

"The doctor at the first hospital said, 'We don't see scorpion babies because they all die,'" Mrs. Bjella stated. In fact, about 1,500 people, mostly children, die in Mexico every year from scorpion stings.

At the suggestion of the doctors, the Bjellas called in an American air ambulance, which flew them to San Diego's Children's Hospital. Anders remained on life support for several days, and the medical intervention proved successful. He recovered, with apparently no permanent aftereffects.

Ants & Ankles

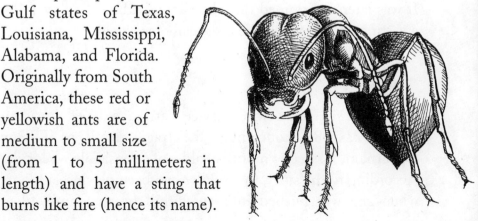

nts are best known as household pests. They swarm into open garbage bags. They form writhing trails between their nests and a single crumb of food left on a kitchen counter. They ruin picnics.

But ants can also cause serious injuries to animals and humans. And in sufficient numbers, some species can even be killers.

The most infamous of these insect pests is the fire ant, found principally in the Gulf states of Texas, Louisiana, Mississippi, Alabama, and Florida. Originally from South America, these red or yellowish ants are of medium to small size (from 1 to 5 millimeters in length) and have a sting that burns like fire (hence its name).

Normally the ant colonies feed on grains and vegetable crops, although they also show a fondness for newly hatched poultry and ground-nesting birds. And every so often they set their sights on something bigger. Like people.

ON APRIL 13, 1994, the Knight-Ridder News Service carried a story guaranteed to give anyone the creeps. According to the report, seventy-seven-year-old Marion Bernhardt of West Palm Beach, Florida, had earlier entered Wellington Regional Hospital for abdominal surgery. On April 2 she repeatedly complained of feeling painful biting sensations on her stomach, symptoms the nurses took to simply be the normal tingling and itching associated with postoperative recovery. Finally, when Bernhardt's complaints became increasingly insistent, the nurses threw back her covers, only to find her bed swarming with fire ants.

"They were all over me, all over my stomach, crawling up my catheter—I let out a roar, 'Good God,'" Bernhardt said. "Everybody in the room flew into chaos trying to get them off me."

Nurses quickly moved Bernhardt out of her first-floor intensive care room, which was then sealed off and fumigated. It was later determined that the victim had suffered over 100 ant stings, from which she eventually recovered.

THE *Mercury News* wire service carried a brief story on March 2, 1988, concerning the tragic death of Tiffany Cheatham, sixteen months old, of Pensacola, Florida. According to the story, the toddler had been playing outdoors when she was pushed into an anthill by the family dog.

Enraged, the ants swarmed all over her, subjecting her to literally hundreds of stings. Apparently the girl then suffered an allergic reaction to the insects' venom and died soon after of anaphylactic shock (see p. 76).

IN THE SUMMER of 1993, a remote Brazilian town experienced a plague straight out of a 1950s horror movie. According to a story circulated nationally by the *Washington Post*, the village of Envira, population 6,800, had found itself besieged by an unstoppable army of fire ants.

The story described a "stereotypical town of barefoot children and wooden houses on stilts on the banks of an Amazon River tributary"—as well as thousands of anthills. The infestation had begun in 1990 and three years later had become a plague of biblical proportions.

"Almost every family has had children attacked," the town's mayor, Luiz Castro, is quoted as saying. Dozens of children were hospitalized due to ant stings, some of which proved fatal. The swarms also killed chickens, ducks, and even turtles.

The fire ants attacked people in their beds while sleeping. They destroyed valuable crops. In the local hospital the legs of beds had to be put in cans filled with water to keep the insects from crawling onto the patients.

When counterattacks ranging from conventional pesticides to diesel fuel and even fire proved useless, the Brazilian government called in a team of entomological (insect) experts from the United States. Although the U.S. team was able to reduce the problem by using poisons specially designed to kill each colony's queen and thus destroy its reproductive system, they admitted that no solution would be permanent.

"It's like taking care of cockroaches," said one of the U.S. team members. "You don't eradicate them; you control them."

At most, the effects of the U.S. effort were expected to last nine months . . . and then the ants would be back.

chapter 10

To Bee Or Not To Bee

We've all heard the term "killer bees." The name dates back to 1957 when Brazilian scientists interbred aggressive African bees with the more docile European honeybee in hopes of increasing the latter's honey-making potential. Unfortunately, a group of these new "Africanized" bees was accidentally released into the wild, and they soon began a slow but steady migration northward, multiplying their numbers a thousandfold and leaving a trail of dead livestock—and humans—in their wake. By the mid-1970s, scientists predicted that these "killer bees" would make their way to the United States by the early 1990s and cause all manner of havoc. Stories about communities being besieged by swarms of lethal bees became the subject of numerous novels, feature films, and made-for-TV movies during the 1970s and 1980s.

Part of the prediction proved correct. Africanized bees *did* reach the southern United States in 1991, but they haven't proven to be the doomsday plague some science-fiction writers imagined.

The fact is, "killer bees" are no more poisonous than conventional honeybees. Their danger lies in their aggressiveness, tendency to swarm, and habit of chasing victims farther than most other bees will. They kill by covering their victims and stinging them dozens, perhaps hundreds of times. The total effect of so much venom causes a human victim's cell membranes to break down, kills red blood cells, and poisons the central nervous system. Five hundred stings are usually enough to destroy a human's kidney function.

Today hives of Africanized bees can be found throughout the southern United States. Many entomologists believe that the bees are slowly interbreeding with native, less aggressive species, and in time their characteristic ferocity will substantially decrease.

THE FIRST RECORDED mass attack by Africanized bees on U.S. soil occurred on June 5, 1991, in the city of Brownsville, Texas, near the Mexican border. The victim was Cenobio Jesus Diaz, a maintenance man working in that city's Siesta Mobile Home Park.

According to a report distributed nationwide by the *Washington Post,* Diaz was riding a lawn mower when he ran over an abandoned drainpipe where the newly arrived bees had apparently built a hive. Swarming over Diaz, they inflicted over 15 stings on his chin, neck, arms, and head before he was able to seek shelter.

Following the incident, several insect bodies were recovered and shipped to the federal government's bee laboratory in Beltsville, Maryland. There, scientists confirmed that the bees were "100 percent Africanized," thus heralding the arrival that had been predicted decades earlier.

THE FIRST CONFIRMED attack by "killer bees" in the state of California occurred nearly four and a half years after their arrival in Texas. On December 30, 1995, the Associated Press reported that a pair of tree trimmers working in Indio, situated just east of Palm Springs, had been attacked by an Africanized swarm.

The two men were clearing branches from power lines when the attack occurred. Camerino Leyva was in a cherry-picker crane about two and a half stories up while his partner, Manuel Corea, was on the ground near the truck. Leyva reportedly cut back a branch, only to have a swarm of bees come pouring out.

The bees massed around Leyva's body and began stinging him. Afraid that, in the confusion, he'd hit the wrong controls and send himself into the electrified power lines, he screamed for his partner to lower him to the ground.

The hydraulically powered crane took two full minutes to retract, during which time the bees kept stinging Leyva. When Corea finally got to the crane, the bees attacked him also. Leyva tried to run, but he still had his safety belt secured, and Corea had to pull him free. Finally the pair ran for shelter, but the bees maintained their attack. Both men found this highly unusual.

"We ran for 200 to 300 yards with 10 or 15 bees following us the whole way," Leyva explained. "I've been stung before, but usually you run 20 yards and you are okay. They kept following."

ANY BEE CAN BE A "KILLER"

Any bee can be a "killer bee" if your genetics are right. About 1 percent of the American population has an inbred sensitivity to bee, wasp, and hornet stings that results in a severe allergic reaction called *anaphylactic shock*. As a result, anywhere from 40 to 80 Americans die from bee stings every year.

Symptoms of anaphylactic shock include abdominal cramping, throat swelling, difficulty breathing, dizziness, and a sudden, steep drop in blood pressure. If the reaction is severe enough, death can occur within minutes.

If you or someone you know is ever stung by a bee and begins to experience any of these symptoms, seek medical help *immediately*. If you know that you suffer from bee-sting allergies, you're advised to wear a medic-alert bracelet indicating this fact. Reactions are so fast that, following a bee sting, you may not be in any condition to tell anyone of your problem. And any delay in treatment could prove fatal.

Leyva and Corea were eventually taken to a local hospital where they were treated and released. In all, Leyva was stung 25 times. Corea suffered 15 stings. In spite of their trauma, both men returned to work the following day.

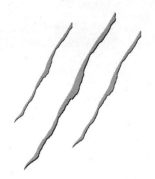

SECTION 4

IN OUR OWN BACKYARDS

Animal Attacks in the Concrete Jungle

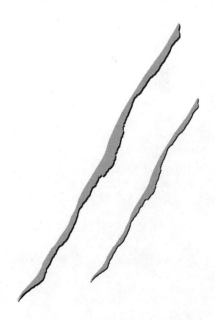

chapter 11

Elephants Never Forget

Because of their great strength, high intelligence, and reputation for docility, elephants have been used as beasts of burden in Asia and Africa for hundreds, if not thousands, of years. Here in the United States, our experience with elephants has mostly been limited to zoos and circuses, where many have been trained to perform a variety of tricks for our amusement.

Because of their great size and thick hides, elephants in the wild have few natural enemies, and thus have evolved into relatively calm, docile animals.

However, if they feel like they or their young are physically threatened, elephants can become as ferocious and destructive as many other jungle beasts.

And when such attacks occur, they inevitably make the evening news.

"HOLIDAY BLUES" USUALLY affect only humans, but on Christmas Eve 1991, a forty-year-old zookeeper working at the Houston Zoological Gardens had his holiday spoiled by one very depressed elephant.

According to an Associated Press report published nationwide the following day, Indu, a 4-ton Asian elephant at the zoo, refused to obey her handler's commands and brutally shoved her way into a small enclosure containing another female elephant and her five-month-old calf. It seems that Indu had lost her own calf in childbirth two months previous, and had been depressed and aggressive ever since.

Indu slammed the other female into a fence, and when her trainer yelled for her to stop, the elephant turned and charged him, breaking his collarbone and four ribs.

A second zookeeper was able to distract the beast long enough for his wounded partner to escape from the enclosure and seek medical treatment.

"It was like a bolt of lightning, it all happened so fast," Red Bayer, the zoo's assistant manager, stated.

Following this attack, an entirely new method of training elephants was instituted at the Houston Zoo, one that rewards the animals with food and social privileges for their "voluntary" cooperation. This new system, which involves less direct contact between elephants and trainers, has since been adopted by many other major zoos throughout the United States.

WHEN PEOPLE GO to a circus, they expect all the danger to be risked by the performers, not themselves. But the 500 people attending Florida's Great American Circus on Saturday, February 1, 1992, faced a life-or-death situation of their own when Kelly, a twenty-seven-year-old Indian elephant, suddenly went wild and attacked the crowd.

According to reports carried in the *Los Angeles Times* and *Chicago Tribune* the following Monday, the 8,000-pound elephant was carrying five children and a woman (all circus performers) on its back when, for no apparent reason, it charged out of the ring. Officer Blayne Doyle, a ten-year police veteran who was working security that day, tried to stop the rampaging pachyderm, only to have it grab him by its trunk, throw him to the ground, and try to stomp him to death. Luckily he was able to reach out and grab an elephant trainer's hook and pull himself to safety.

"I thought I was dead," Doyle stated. "I've never been scared as much as I was then."

The animal reportedly then attacked two parked circus trucks and a crowded circus tent. Panicked spectators ran in all directions and clogged an exit door, which the elephant then set its sights on.

With no tranquilizer guns available, police on the scene had no choice but to use their handguns. They unloaded a volley of bullets at the elephant, bringing it down before hundreds of horrified spectators. In all, the elephant took 25 bullets before succumbing and collapsed only 15 to 20 yards from the trapped visitors.

Investigators could find no clear reason for the elephant's suddenly aberrant behavior.

MANY ELEPHANT ATTACKS occur on the elephants' native soil, and when they do, the results can be catastrophic. For example, on August 29, 1993, both Reuters and the *Chicago Tribune* wire services reported that at least 44 people had been killed by a rogue elephant stampeding through three villages in Assam, a state in the northeastern section of India.

The elephant, perhaps enraged by the expansion of humans into its perceived territory, smashed through the villages of Thelamara, Muslim Char, and Butamari, smashing homes and trampling terrified villagers underfoot. Citizens in the area posted all-night sentries and burned torches in hopes of keeping the killer away.

Government officials used five trained marksmen to finally locate and destroy the rampaging beast.

From 1988 to 1993 more than 100 people were killed in elephant attacks throughout India.

chapter 12

When Pets Strike Back

Ve take animals into our homes for companionship, security, and even love. We feed them, bathe them, train them to obey commands, and generally treat them like members of the family. The death of a pet is often akin to the death of a loved one.

Scientists now believe that dogs and man have enjoyed a symbiotic relationship that goes back almost 10,000 years. Cats were highly prized in Ancient Egypt, and birds have been used for both hunting and ornamentation throughout the world since the dawn of history.

But what we often forget is that animals are, well, animals, and they'll often revert to instinctive behaviors, even if it means literally biting the hands that feed them. Pet owners who ignore this simple fact do so at their own peril.

AS WITH SPIDERS, many people have an instinctive fear of snakes. But there are others who not only enjoy the company of these legless reptiles, they eagerly invite them into their homes as pets. And snakes *can* make interesting, exotic housemates. However, when the snake is a Burmese python and its size gets beyond 6 feet, the results can be downright dangerous, as these numerous reports from around the nation suggest.

> On October 9, 1996, nineteen-year-old Grant Williams of the Bronx was found strangled to death in his apartment. The killer wasn't some burglar or street thug but the teen's own 13-foot-long, 44-pound pet python that he'd recently purchased for $300. According to reports carried in the *New York Times,* the *Boston Globe,* and *Jet* magazine, Williams normally fed the snake live rabbits but had decided to try a live chicken on the day of the attack. The smell of the chicken had apparently driven the snake into a homicidal frenzy, and it attacked Williams rather than the hen. His body was discovered by a next-door neighbor facedown, with blood coming from his mouth. Rescue workers were able to remove the snake from Williams's body and rush him to a nearby hospital, where he died an hour later of "asphyxia due to compression of the neck by the snake."

> On Saturday, August 31, 1996, the *Boston Globe* reported that an 8-foot pet python that was out of its cage found seven-

year-old Cory Berard of Cranston, Rhode Island, playing with his pet hamster. The snake reportedly wrapped itself around the boy and bit his left hand and forearm, then bit the boy's aunt, Patricia Grenon, when she tried to come to his aid. (Pythons, unlike rattlesnakes, are nonvenomous.) A city animal control officer was able to remove the snake, which was taken to a local animal shelter, while both Cory and his aunt were treated at a local hospital.

A story published by the *Chicago Tribune* on November 6, 1994, described how a 13-foot, 30-pound python residing at a home on the city's northeast side had escaped from its cage, slithered into the house's basement, and attacked a four-year-old boy who was playing with several friends. When the other boys were unable to remove the snake, which had coiled itself around the terrified boy's body, firefighters were called in. "We took some shears, cut the [snake's] neck, then hit him in the head with an ax," one of the attending officers explained.

On May 18, 1993, the *Chicago Tribune* reported the untimely death of William Bassett, forty-seven, of Harahan, Louisiana. Bassett, who reportedly owned at least 11 snakes, had been crushed to death, presumably on May 14, by one of his pets, a 16-foot, 200-pound python. Wounds on the snake and other evidence at the scene suggested that Bassett had attempted to kill his assailant with a kitchen knife before succumbing to asphyxiation.

Tom Ortiz, twenty-four, of Kansas City, Missouri, barely escaped death when his 15-foot pet python, Tina, wrapped itself around his body and attempted to squeeze him to death. Although he eventually fell unconscious, paramedics arrived just in time to free him from the snake's grasp and resuscitate him, according to a story carried by the Associated Press on July 3, 1989.

Richard Hull, twenty-three, and his girlfriend, Kathy Cramer, twenty-six, had been house-sitting for a friend near San Francisco during early 1986. Their responsibilities included taking care of Monty, the owner's 12-foot pet python. They'd come to trust the snake, so much so that they let it sleep with them. According to a report carried by the Associated Press on April 7, 1986, Hull and Cramer had two friends over when Cramer went to feed Monty a live rabbit. At that point the snake leaped from its cage and attacked her instead. "I heard her yell 'Richard!' " Hull told reporters. "I ran into the room and the snake had Kathy around the neck and all wrapped around her face and head." Unable to pull the snake free, Hull and his friends were forced to cut the serpent's head off with a kitchen knife. Cramer was later treated for minor bite wounds. She later told reporters that Monty had been "real moody" after it had shed its skin. "Oh, yeah, I was kind of scared," she stated. "But I'm really sorry we had to kill him because he was a beautiful snake."

PIT BULLS WERE bred for fighting. Although most of these stocky, muscular dogs are today kept as house pets that cause no trouble whatsoever, the inescapable fact remains that their genetic legacy is that of an aggressive pit fighter, one designed not only to attack a perceived enemy but to continue fighting to the death. The growing popularity of pit bulls as domestic pets in recent years has resulted in a proportionately larger number of attacks attributed to these animals.

Here are just a few of literally dozens of recent incidents.

On Sunday, February 12, 1995, the *San Jose Mercury News* reported that police were searching for the owner of two female pit bulls that had randomly attacked pedestrians in Sausalito, just north of San Francisco, the previous Friday. According to the article, the two dogs began attacking people on a busy street corner that night. A startled bystander reportedly hit one of the dogs across the head with a crowbar, with no visible effect. Police soon arrived and one officer shot the other dog with his 9 mm pistol. Both dogs merely fled down the street. They were finally cornered at the top of a staircase and held there until they could be removed by city animal control officers. In all, four people had to be treated for bite wounds, several of them serious.

On October 3, 1991, the *San Jose Mercury News* carried a report of what was described as one of the worst dog maulings in the history of the U.S. Postal Service. According to the story, Joel Akot, a thirty-six-year-old mail carrier, was filling in for another postal worker along a route that took him to a duplex on North 11th Street in San Jose. He had just finished delivering the mail when he heard a snarling noise behind him. Rex, a five-year-old male pit bull that belonged to the unit's resident, Janet Olivera, smashed through the home's screen door, bit Akot's thigh, and then went for his arm.

"He was biting real hard," Akot later said. "I was trying to reach the dog's neck. The mailbag dropped. I saw my [pepper] spray, I reached for it, and sprayed the dog. Then he released my arm."

At the hospital Akot was treated for bite wounds to his thigh, arm, and stomach. Olivera, who reportedly got the dog from her late brother who was murdered earlier that year, explained that she kept the dog for protection in a "tough neighborhood" and that it was the smell of Akot's leather mailbag, not Akot himself, that the dog responded to. "It wasn't him personally," she told the Mercury News. "It's the bag he hates."

In June 1987 a camera crew from Los Angeles's KCBS-TV decided to follow a local animal control officer on his rounds to tape a story about aggressive dogs. As reported by the Associated Press on June 23, 1987, the news crew followed animal control officer Florence Crowell to a Glendale-area home as she went to investigate the reported attack on a man and his seven-year-old daughter the previous Sunday by a pit bull named Benjamin, which was owned by their neighbor Joy Hauser. As Crowell and the news crew approached the Hauser home, Benjamin smashed through the house's screen door and clamped its powerful jaws over the officer's hand.

Hauser claimed that Crowell provoked the attack by taunting the animal. "I did not sic Benjamin on her," the owner insisted. "[Crowell] was standing at the edge of the driveway, crunched over and waving a stick. I told her that she better be careful because Benjamin would attack if she kept waving a stick." The dog abandoned its attack only after a helpful neighbor was able to beat it off with a stick of her own. As for the KCBS-TV camera crew, they got an unintended exclusive for the six o'clock news.

On December 13, 1988, the *Akron Beacon Journal* reported that six-month-old Amber Haverstock had been killed by Spike, her family's five-year-old, 60-pound pit bull. According to the report, the attack occurred after Amber's mother, Carrie Vergara, split a cookie in two, giving one half to the infant girl, who was sitting in a walker, and the other half to Spike. The dog then went for the baby, apparently in an attempt to get the other half of the cookie for himself. The 24-pound infant later died of cardiovascular collapse caused by numerous bite injuries. In particular, her spleen was torn in two and there was massive kidney damage, resulting in widespread internal bleeding.

"I have heard of deaths like this, but I never expected to see injuries so severe," Summit County Coroner Dr. William Cox stated. "A few years ago, I saw injuries that were caused when a child was attacked by a tiger. Those injuries pale in comparison to this girl."

DOGS AREN'T THE only normally docile house pets that can turn nasty. In July 1995 the town of Rumford, Rhode Island, was terrorized by two stray cats, both of which were believed to be carrying rabies. According to a report distributed nationally by the Associated Press on July 15, 1995, the cats tended to attack humans and house pets who were walking outdoors. The first victim was Bill Mahoney, who was attacked on July 3. He was preparing to water his lawn when a small gray cat jumped on him, gouged his arms with its claws, then chased him for several blocks before finally giving up.

Charline Ritinski and her fox terrier, Walter, were another set of victims. "I was walking down Greenwood Avenue and then, all of a sudden, it was on my dog's head like some kind of alien," Ritinski stated, describing the same small gray cat that had attacked Mahoney. The cat reportedly wrapped its front legs around the dog's neck and its hind legs around the animal's stomach, biting and clawing the entire time. The dog managed to dislodge its attacker by banging the cat's head against a guardrail.

All the victims, including a nine-year-old girl and a seventy-three-year-old man, were given rabies shots and were released in apparently good condition. Animal control officers said traps and a mass eradication of stray cats in the Rumford area was launched as a result of the attacks.

chapter  13

Where They Don't Belong

Every now and then, normally "wild" animals wind up in places they don't belong. In 1995 TV viewers in the Los Angeles area were delighted by a series of home videos showing a native black bear that decided to frequent the hot tub of a home in the city's northern foothills. Moose have been known to occasionally show up on the Main Streets of several New England cities.

But while many of these "fish-out-of-water"—or "moose-out-of-forest"—stories are amusing, others are downright serious, especially when the animal in question is a known predator. And even normally benign moose can become killers when provoked.

Here are some recent incidents involving people who have confronted some of nature's fiercest killers in places they never expected.

ON SEPTEMBER 11, 1994, the *San Jose Mercury News* carried a story about a mountain lion stalking the campus of Stanford University in nearby Palo Alto. "It was sauntering along like it owned the area," stated Lori Kratzer, a fifteen-year police veteran who was one of several people who spotted the cougar on Junipero Serra Boulevard at around 7:40 Saturday morning. Although a one-and-a-half-hour-long search for the big cat was subsequently launched, it was not seen again. Ironically, this was the same weekend that the Northwestern Wildcats football team was in town to play football.

IN A LESS amusing incident, a stray mountain lion was shot and killed by police just outside the heavily traveled Montclair Plaza shopping mall in Montclair, California, east of Los Angeles, on August 23, 1994. The *Mercury News* wire service reported the following day that the two- to three-year-old cat was cornered beneath a vehicle in the mall's parking lot and shot with a tranquilizer dart. However, when the cougar emerged and charged one of the officers, it was shot dead.

ON JANUARY 15, 1995, several news sources, including *USA Today*, the Associated Press, and the *Los Angeles Times*, reported the death of seventy-one-year-old Myong Chin Ra at the University of Alaska's Anchorage campus. According to the reports, a female moose and her calf had wandered onto the campus from the nearby woods and were harassed by students who threw snowballs at them for several hours. Enraged, the moose first went for a professor, then stomped Ra to death when he tried to walk past them.

ON JULY 29, 1994, sixty-four-year-old Donald L. Mathews poked his head up into the attic of his Leona Valley home, situated 35 miles north of Los Angeles, only to be bit in the neck by a rattlesnake. Found by his wife, Betty, suffering from an extremely swollen neck and chest, Mathews was flown to Antelope Valley Hospital where he was listed in critical condition.

The snake lunged "so fast [Mathews] probably didn't even know what happened until it was too late," stated Capt. Ron Hamilton of the Los Angeles Fire Department in a story carried nationally by the Associated Press two days later.

Animal control officers captured the 18-inch-long snake later that evening.

"It was a very unhappy snake," Betty Mathews told the AP.

ANOTHER SURPRISE SNAKEBITE was suffered by Edward N. Cullom of San Jose, California, when he reached down to pick up a plant at a local Wal-Mart store, only to be bit on the hand by a 14-inch pygmy rattlesnake. At first he thought he had merely pricked his finger on a thorn but then pulled his hand back to see the snake still hanging off the end of his finger. In the story carried by the *Mercury News* wire service on August 20, 1987, Cullom was reportedly taken to a nearby hospital suffering from blurred vision, nausea, and a swollen hand. Wal-Mart officials promised to take "appropriate actions," presumably against the snake.

IN PERHAPS ONE of the oddest suicides on record, the Associated Press carried a story on June 9, 1987, reporting that Mark W. Johnson, thirty-eight, of Riverside County, California, had apparently decided to deal with a shattered romance by allowing a rattlesnake to bite him repeatedly on the hand. Johnson kept several venomous snakes in his home as pets, and feeling despondent over a recent breakup with his girlfriend, apparently decided to use one to end his life. Johnson suffered cardiac arrest while en route to the hospital. He was given a horse-serum snakebite treatment but proved to be allergic to the medication. He died of his wounds five hours later.

Index